Blue Poison Dart Frog

This little frog is easy to spot. But most **predators** will not try to eat it. The frog's bright colors say, "Watch out! I'm full of poison."

Indigo Bunting

Some animals want to send out a different message. Their blue bodies say, "Come to me!"

This bird's bright feathers help him **attract** a mate. The female's feathers are light brown. They help her hide from predators.

Blue-Footed Boobies

At mating time, these birds put on an amazing show. The male spreads his wings wide and whistles. Then he struts, slides, shuffles, and stomps his bright blue feet. That's one good way to get a female to look at him!

Golden Monkeys

These monkeys live in mountain forests. Their light brown fur makes them hard to spot. Luckily, they know how to find one another. They just look for the bright blue faces of their family and friends.

Morpho Butterfly

The tops of this butterfly's wings really stand out, but the bottoms are light brown. When the insect rests with its wings folded up, it is very hard to see. If a predator gets too close, the butterfly snaps its wings open. The blue flash surprises the predator. That gives the butterfly a chance to get away.

Blue-Tongued Skink

This lizard has its own trick for staying safe. When an enemy attacks, the lizard sticks out its tongue. The bright color helps scare off the predator.

Blue Darner Dragonfly

This insect can change the color of its body. On cool mornings, it is dark blue. That helps its body warm up faster in the sun. On hot afternoons, the dragonfly turns light blue. That helps its body cool off.

Guessing Game

Being blue helps many kinds of animals stay alive. It helps some animals send a message to mates or predators. It helps other animals hide from their enemies. How do you think being blue helps the animals in these photos?

green bottle blue tarantula

(See answers on page 32.)

Where Do These Blue

Animals Live?

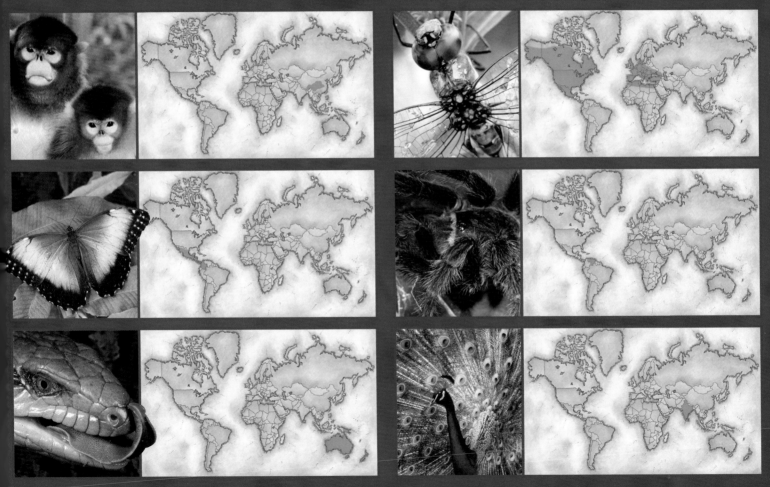

Learn More

Books

Jenkins, Steve. *Living Color*. Boston: Houghton Mifflin, 2007.

Kalman, Bobbie, and John Crossingham. *Camouflage: Changing to Hide*. New York: Crabtree Publishing, 2005.

Smith, Molly. *Blue Whale: The World's Biggest Mammal*. New York: Bearport Publishing, 2007.

Stockland, Patricia M. *Red Eyes or Blue Feathers: A Book About Animal Colors*. Minneapolis, Minn.: Picture Window Books, 2005.

Whitehouse, Patricia. *Colors We Eat: Purple and Blue Foods*. Chicago: Heinemann, 2004.

The Life of
Ben Franklin

By Maria Nelson

Gareth Stevens
Publishing

Please visit our website, www.garethstevens.com. For a free color catalog of all our high-quality books, call toll free 1-800-542-2595 or fax 1-877-542-2596.

Library of Congress Cataloging-in-Publication Data

Nelson, Maria.
The life of Ben Franklin / Maria Nelson.
    p. cm. — (Famous lives)
Includes index.
ISBN 978-1-4339-6347-6 (pbk.)
ISBN 978-1-4339-6348-3 (6-pack)
ISBN 978-1-4339-6345-2 (library binding)
1. Franklin, Benjamin, 1706-1790—Juvenile literature. 2. Statesmen—United States—Biography—Juvenile literature. 3. Inventors—United States—Biography—Juvenile literature. 4. Scientists—United States—Biography—Juvenile literature. 5. Printers—United States—Biography—Juvenile literature. I. Title.
E302.6.F8N45 2012
973.3092—dc23
[B]
                                2011019786

First Edition

Published in 2012 by
Gareth Stevens Publishing
111 East 14th Street, Suite 349
New York, NY 10003

Copyright © 2012 Gareth Stevens Publishing

Designer: Daniel Hosek
Editor: Kristen Rajczak

Photo credits: Cover, pp. 1, 5, 17, 21 Stock Montage/Getty Images; pp. 7, 9, 11 Kean Collection/ Getty Images; p. 13 Hulton Archive/Getty Images; p. 15 Time Life Pictures/Getty Images; p. 19 Roger Viollet Collection/Getty Images.

Printed in the United States of America

CPSIA compliance information: Batch #CW12GS: For further information contact Gareth Stevens, New York, New York at 1-800-542-2595.

Learn More

Web Sites

Animal Colors

http://www.highlightskids.com/Science/Stories/SS1000_
animalColors.asp

Beasts Playground: Camouflage Game

http://www.abc.net.au/beasts/playground/camouflage.htm

How Animal Camouflage Works

http://science.howstuffworks.com/animal-camouflage.htm

Index

Enslow Elementary, an imprint of Enslow Publishers, Inc.

Enslow Elementary® is a registered trademark of Enslow Publishers, Inc.

Copyright © 2009 by Melissa Stewart

All rights reserved.

No part of this book may be reproduced by any means without the written permission of the publisher.

Library of Congress Cataloging-in-Publication Data

Stewart, Melissa.

Why are animals blue? / Melissa Stewart.

p. cm. — (Rainbow of animals)

Includes bibliographical references.

Summary: "Uses examples of animals in the wild to explain why some animals are blue"— Provided by publisher.

ISBN 978-0-7660-3251-4

1. Animals—Color—Juvenile literature. 2. Blue—Juvenile literature. I. Title.

QL767.S745 2009

591.47'2—dc22   2008011469

ISBN-10: 0-7660-3251-5

Printed in the United States of America

10 9 8 7 6 5 4 3 2 1

All photos by Minden Pictures:

Interior: © Barry Mansell/npl, p. 5 (frog); © Birgitte Wilms, pp. 10–11, 28 (octopus); © Chris Newbert, p. 4 (boxfish); © Frans Lanting, pp. 1 (bottom left), 5 (katydid), 26 (right), 29 (peacock); © Greg Harold/Auscape, pp. 22–23, 29 (skink); © Hans Cristoph Kappel/npl, p. 5 (butterfly); © Heidi & Hans-Jurgen Koch, pp. 26 (left), 29 (tarantula); © Ingo Arndt/Foto Natura, p. 21 (inset); © Michael & Patricia Fogden, pp. 1 (top left), 3, 12–13, 20–21, 28 (frog), 29 (butterfly); © Norbert Wu, pp. 8–9, 28 (shark); © Pete Oxford, p. 4 (chameleon); © Tim Fitzharris, pp. 1 (bottom right), 24–25, 29 (dragonfly); © Tom Vezo, p. 4 (cardinal), 14–15, 28 (bunting); © Tui De Roy, pp. 6-7, 16–17, 28 (blue-footed boobies), 28 (heron); © ZSSD, pp. 18–19, 29 (monkeys).

Cover: (clockwise from top left) © Michael & Patricia Fogden; © Frans Lanting; © Tim Fitzharris; © Michael & Patricia Fogden.

Illustration Credits: © 1999, Artville, LLC, pp. 28–29 (maps).

Note to Parents and Teachers: The *Rainbow of Animals* series supports the National Science Education Standards for K–4 science. The Words to Know section introduces subject-specific vocabulary words, including pronunciation and definitions. Early readers may need help with these new words.

Answers to the Guessing Game:

The dark blue and green body of a green bottle blue tarantula helps it hide in shadows.

The bright blue body and huge tail of a peacock help it attract a mate.

Enslow Elementary
an imprint of
Enslow Publishers, Inc.
40 Industrial Road
Box 398
Berkeley Heights, NJ 07922
USA
http://www.enslow.com